WILD ORCHIDS

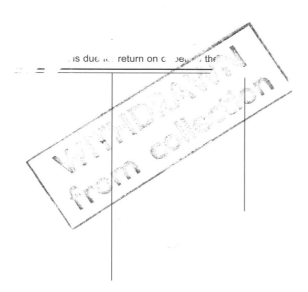

...is due for return on or before the...

ULIA GIBSON

D1464644

Published in 2009 by Antony Rowe Publishing
48-50 Birch Close
Eastbourne
East Sussex
BN23 6PE
arp@cpi-group.co.uk

A catalogue record for this book is available from the British Library

ISBN - 9781905200757

Printed and Bound in Great Britain by
CPI Antony Rowe, Chippenham and Eastbourne

contents

my thanks to

Geoffrey Sheargold: without whose knowledge and enthusiasm I would not have located these threatened plants. Adam and Oli for their valuable ideas and their young gifts. Sarah Lee for giving her spare time proof reading. Geoffrey Wood botanist at Kew Gardens for confirming Latin/ Greek meanings.Veronica Gates Surrey Wildlife Trust for your advice and encouragement.
To the Surrey Wildlife Trust for facilitating my wildlife photographs to be published in the Surrey Nature. David Leedham for his skills of producing my photographic web site.

juliagibsonphotos.co.uk.

Introduction

This book is to show the Wild Orchids of Surrey in their natural habitat, their different stages of growth (where possible) and their common and latin names and meanings (where known). Throughout Britain there are many species and locations of Orchid, such as in the Hebridian Isles, Pembrokeshire, Dorset, Devon, Co. Mayo, Co. Clare and Kent, among other locations. Orchids grow in an array of diverse habitats, such as, fly ash tips, road verges, pinewoods, beech woodland, low montane, moorland, bogs, fens, marshes, limestone, dune stacks, machair and grassland. There are laws and policies in place in both the UK and Ireland to safeguard endangered wild plants. I have therefore not written where these endangered plants have been photographed. Local Wildlife Trusts have established Sites of Natural Conservation Interest (SNCI), some of which contain orchid habitats.

Julia Gibson has been a keen and successful photographer for 10 years since her first travels to Africa which took her to see places and animals that inspired her creative art form of wildlife photography.
She lives in Surrey and is a keen walker and this has inspired her love of the British country side with its diverse fauna and flora.
For a number of years her photographs have been sold in exhibitions and she is a regular photographer for the Surrey Wildlife Trust, an organisation which preserves and restores our fragile ecosystem.
Surrey Wildlife Trust is celebrating its 50th anniversary in 2009.

orchis mascula EARLY PURPLE

40cms 15 inches high flowers in Early May
Orchid Greek for testicle in reference to the tuber.
Mascula means male.

In early March the first orchid of the season to be found are these
extraordinary orchid species.From the moment they begin to emerge
you are in for a few weeks of drama! Starting with just a few shiny
spotted leaves,returning weekly you gradually see the emergence of
five large spotted glossy leaves. In May a tiny green shoot emerges
with a hint of purple.These stalks quickly grow week by week,
revealing a large shoot of deep purple,until at last the final head of the
flower forms into a perfect Orchid. Growing in wooded areas amidst
ancient Yews they are typically hidden amongst last year's fallen
leaves.

4

8

neottia nidus-avis BIRDS NEST ORCHID

25cms 10 inches high flowers early May
Greek Neotteia a birds nest in reference to untidy fleshy roots

A plain, some would even say a dull orchid, of light brown colour,
seen growing next to the previous years dried flower. Obscured in low
light next to the base of ancient Yew trees is rarely seen. Standing at
25 cms high is usually found in small groups. As the orchid grows
through the stem over 2-3 weeks the flower buds emerge through
fallen brown leaves left from the previous year's autumn, before
flowering. This orchid has rhizome roots, which look like bird nests in
appearance,hence its name. Tree roots are connected to the orchid
via fungi threads, known as (tripartite).

orchis anthropophora MAN ORCHID

15-40 cms 16 inches high flowers early May
Latin for man human referring to the lip shape.

These orchid mainly seen in the south east of England is shaped as
a man, as the name suggests. An extraordinary orchid containing
many pale yellow man shaped flowers with dark red edging. The
'hood' is made up of sepals and petals. Found in large groups
underneath hedgerows on steep chalk slopes,making this one of the
most difficult orchids to find. Its unique appearance is truly amazing.
Little is known of its germination process, the flower can have a long
life span of up to 14 years.

plantanthera chlorantha GREATER BUTTERFLY

40 cms 16 inches high flowers end May
Latin Platys broad
Latin chlorantha green flower

So called because of the two sepals which resemble wings. This
beautiful tall, white flower with a long green lip is visited by moths for
pollination. Found in grassy woodland edges with little source of ligh
therefore, does not depend on photosynthesis, but may use fungi for
nutrients. It has a vegetable cycle of up to 2-3 years, followed by a
flowering year to show beautiful white flowers.

neottia listeria ovata COMMON TWAYBLADE

20-60 cms upto 2 ft high flowers mid May
Ovata latin oval shape
Listera relates to Dr Martin Lister 1638-1711 an English naturalist.

A tall and slender plant, has two large broad leaves, a dominant
feature of the plant. The flower is similar to the musk orchid in
appearance with a long forked lip but unlike the Man orchid has a hint
of purple. Found typically in shaded areas at the base of trees.
Underground this plant has rhizomes. In early spring the flower grows
and the first to appear are the two large leaves, from this leaves a tall
slim stem grows,from which multiple buds open within 3-4 weeks.

cephalanthera damasonium WHITE HELLEBORINE

25 cms 10 inches high flowers mid May
Anthera referring to the stipitate head shaped anther.
Latin cephal head.
Greek kephale a head
Latin damaso a derivative to subdue evil as the plant was considered an antidote to the venom of toads.

Found in woodland areas suggesting it to be dependant on fungi for survival -tripartite. This pretty white goblet shaped flower stands erect with only a few flowers on its stem, some of which may not open. The leaves which appear to climb up the stem to be close to the flowers are of a narrow long shape. Self pollinating, it attracts insects.

dactylariza praetermissa SOUTHERN MARSH ORCHID

70 cms 28 inches high flowering in May June.
Latin dactyl finger riza root
Praetermissa latin name for the species.

This broad orchid resembles a cross between the spotted and the Early Purple, light to deep purple it has three lobed lips. Found in water meadows it grows in calcareous soil. Its glossy narrow leaves grow from the base of the stem. Pollinated by butterflies who have been seen picking at the pollinia.

dactylorhiza fuchii COMMON SPOTTED ORCHID

30 cms 1ft high flowers early June
Latin dact y finger
Rhiza Root Fuchs German Botanist Leonard Fuchs(1501-66) after
whom the Fuchia is named.

Identified by long slender pale blotchy green leaves grow up the stem
amongst the flowers. Distinguishable from the Early Purple by the
spotted florets and a paler purple flower.The lips having three folds,
marked with darker purple spots. It flowers after the Early Purple
orchid in early June. The orchid buds blossom into a mass of delicate
flowers found primarily in grassland until the end of July. It can grow i
differing soils, allowing it to spread and self cultivate in many parts of
the county and is therefore the most common of wild orchids in
Britain.

38

orphrys apifera BEE ORCHID

25 cms 10 inches high flowers mid June
Latin Aifera bee shape.
Orphys Greek for an eyebrow may be a reference to the arched dorsa
sepal.

Arguably the most exquisite of all the wild orchids, small delicate and
rich in colours of yellow and purple. The flowers resembles its name
sake, the bumble bee, attracting male bees for pollination in warm
climates possible by it'scolour, as it has no nectar! In Britain the
flower self pollinates, from pollinia to stigmas. Found in small group
on grassland in May with 3-4 flowers on each stem, it can be difficult
to spot as it does not flower every year, flowering only every 2 to 3 yea

gymnadenia conopsea FRAGRANT ORCHID

15-30 cms up to 1ft high flowers mid June
Greek Gymnos naked, aden,a gland from the Pollinia.
Conopsea means knat like or cloudy origin unknown.

So called for its scent, this pale purple orchid is relatively tall by
comparison with other wild orchids. It has multiple unspotted flowers,
looks similar to the Early Purple Orchid. It is visited by butterflies and
moths attracted by the colour and nectar which transfer Pollinia
between flowers.The long Spur (extended lip) facilitate insects only
with long proboscis, therefore restricting many other insect species.
This flower can be easily found in large groups in short grass land
slopes.

herminium monorchis MUSK ORCHID

10cms 4 inches high flowers mid to end June
Latin mono one referring to single tuber
Latin Hermineus white like ermine possibly referring to whiteness of
the flowers of the non British species.

This tiny pale yellow orchids is under real threat, if only because it is
so very easily missed under foot! In full flower it holds 20-30 flowers
on its stems, and stands at just 10 cm. The Musk orchid is easily
camouflaged in grass. Its scent is sweet like honey not musk. Insects
visit and pollinate the plant and the seeds fall in August. Flowering
depends on the last years wet season, they thrive in cool damp
climates and therefore the tubers play an important part by storing
food to guarantee flowering each year.

anacamptis pyramidalis PYRAMIDAL ORCHID

20 cms 8 inches high flowers early July
Greek Anakamptein to bend back in allusion to the volucral bracts
bent back to the tip.
Pyramidalis pyramid shape Greek referring to the pyramid shape
before all the flowers open.

It is not known why insects visit this orchid as it has no nectar in its
spurs, (according to Darwin)! This beautiful deep purple plant stands
tall and slim, found in large groups flowering later than most other
wild orchids from early July. A popular orchid probably because it is
so easy to find. Cross-pollinated by butterflies and moths who
transfer the Pollinia. They have underground tubers. Produces leaves
starting in the autumn.

epipactis purpura VIOLET HELLEBORINE

20-90 cms 3 ft high flowers early August
Epipactis Latin for swampy ground habitat.
Purpurata Latin purplish.

With pale green sepals and petals and pale violet lip its shape is
similar to the Broad leafed Helleborine. The dark green leaves appear
to climb up between each flower. Found in open area, depends on
photosynthesis, therefore, less dependent on fungi than other
Helleborine Orchids.This lovely flower stands erect and tall.

epipactis helleborine BROAD LEAFED HELLEBORINE

40cms16 inches high flowers early August
Greek Epipaktis rupturewort an ancient name for a plant of uncertain identity.

This single narrow stemmed flower has large green leaves resembling those of a Twayblade, only more numerous. The sepals and petals of pale green with pink and rich deep purple containing alcohol fuelled nectar, from which the insects drink! This orchid grows near wooded areas particularly near beech and birch trees. Similar to the birds nest orchid in as much as it uses tree roots and fungi for nutrients. This orchid flowers later than most others in late July and August.

spiranthes spiralis AUTUMN LADY TRESSES

10 cms 4 inches high flowers end August
Spiralis latin for twisted or spiral
Greek Anthos flower

This is the last orchid in the season to flower. It has a uniqueness of shape,as the name suggests it resembles lady braids and forms a white spiral shape. Pollinated by insects, it has a sweet scent and is found on south facing slopes. Underground the tubers grow vertically to become invaded by fungi for food storage. Grows in short open grassland, this remarkably small and delicate flower with a very different and interesting appearance.

glossary

BRACT
A small leaf at the base of a stem
MYCORRHIZA
Root plant relationship, greek for root, the fungus colonises the root
the host in turn providing the fungus with carbohydrates produced by
the plant in photosynthesis.
ECHOMYCORRHIZA
Form between wooded plants and fungi e.g. bird nest orchids.
PHOTOSYNTHESIS
Plant convert carbon dioxide into organic compounds e.g. sucrose
from light to use as a source of energy.
RHIZOME
Horizontal stem of the plant usually form underground.
STAMEN
Male organ of the plant.
EPIPHYTES
Plants that anchor on to other plant or shrubs.
PHEROMONES
Chemicals which contain sexual attractant properties.
SPURS
Lip extension where nectar collects.
PROBOSCIS
Insects tool for collecting nectar.
TRIPARTITE
A plant which is dependant on three organic materials e.g. trees
fungi,flowers.
STIGMA
Receives pollen during pollination connected the to ovary (female
gland).
CALCAREOUS SOIL
Sedimentary alkaline soil of calcium carbonate,also good for growing
vines.
TUBERS
Thick underground food-stores.